SUMMMER
FASHION
COLORING BOOK

THE BEST COLORING BOOK
FOR GIRLS WHO LOVE FASHION!

32 PAGES TO COLOR
SWIMWEAR
COVER-UPS
ACCESSORIES

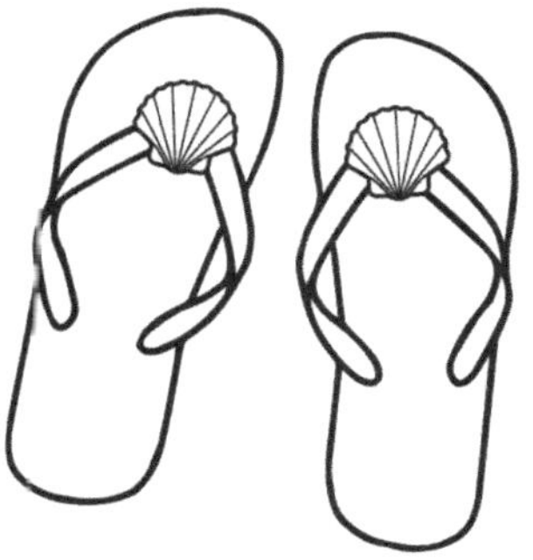

+DESIGN YOUR OWN
SWIMWEAR &
ACCESORIES

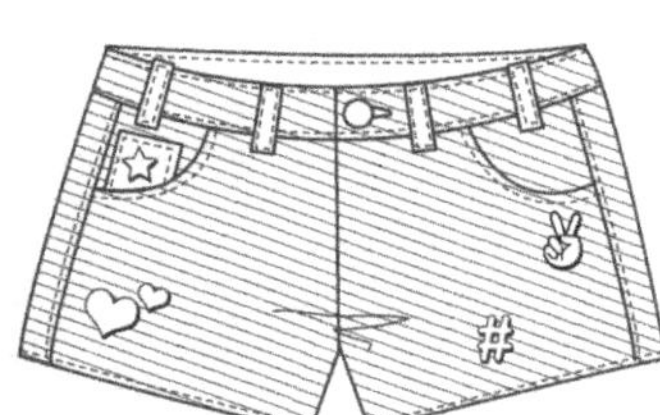

DESIGNED BY DANI KATES

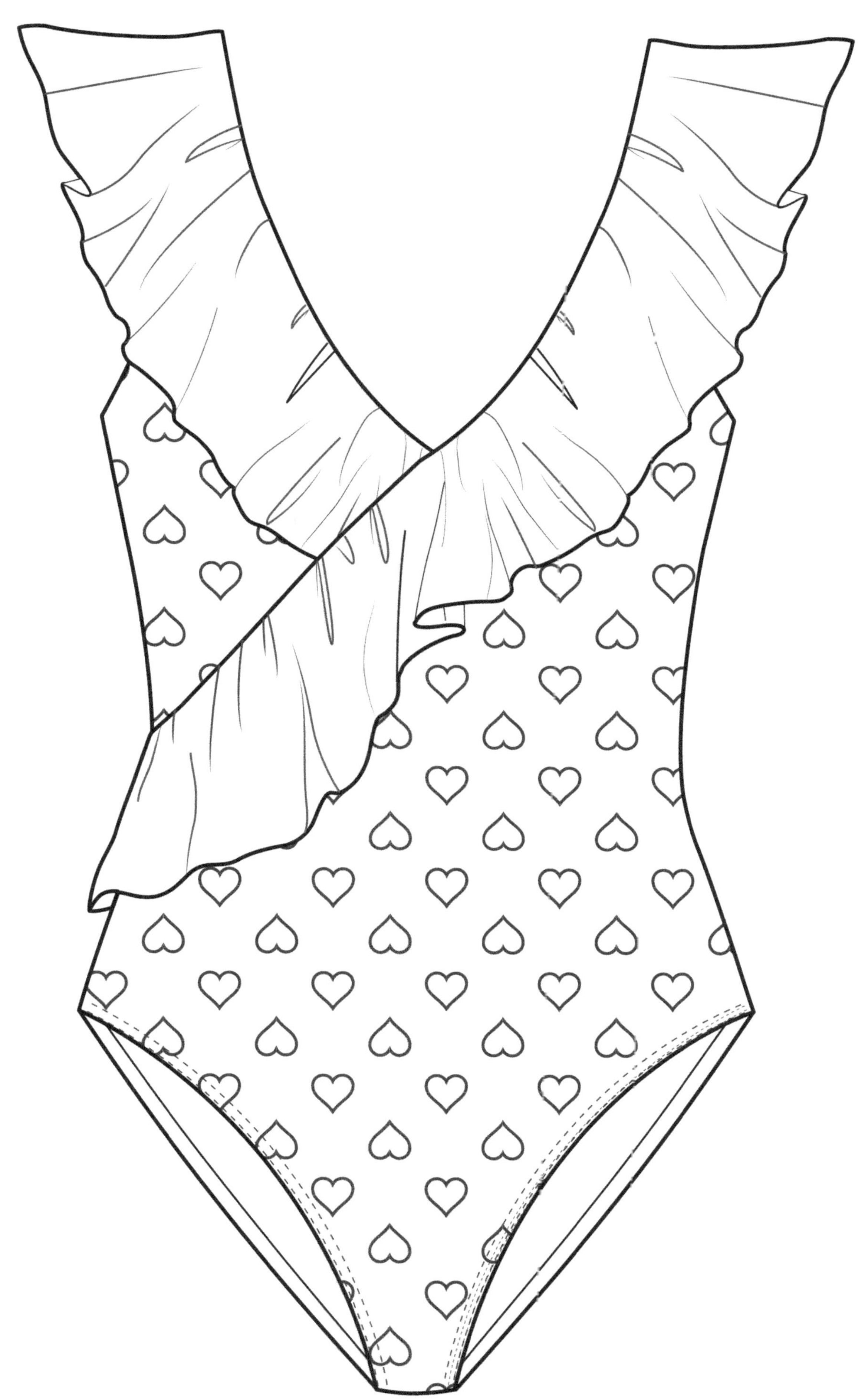

MERMAID
OFF DUTY

HELLO
SUMMER

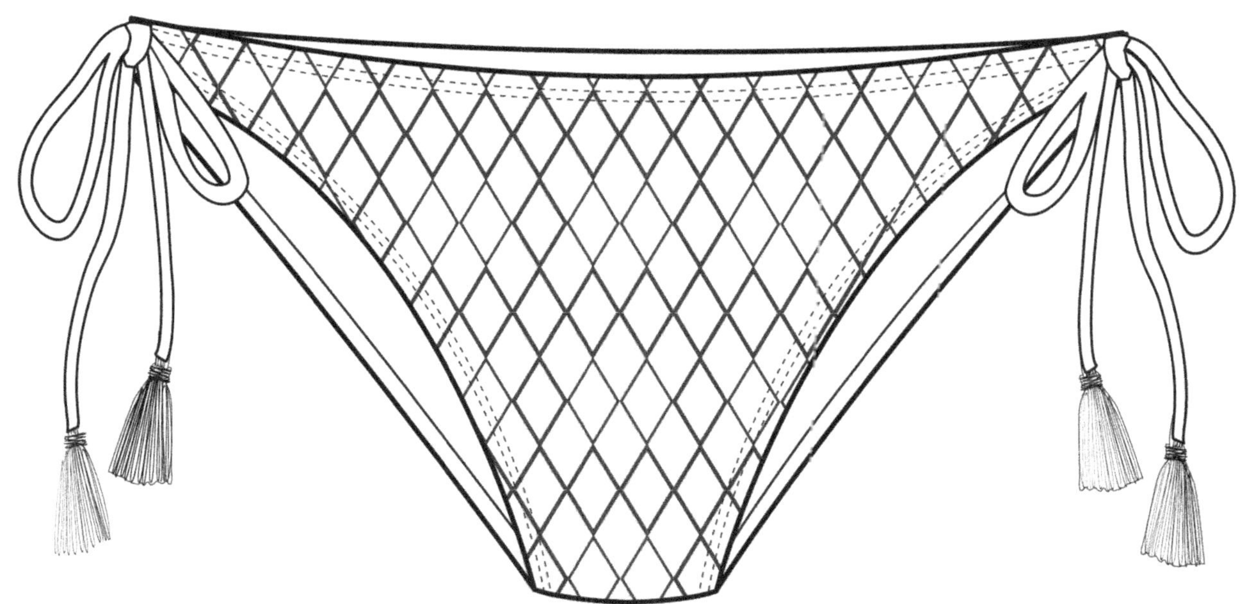

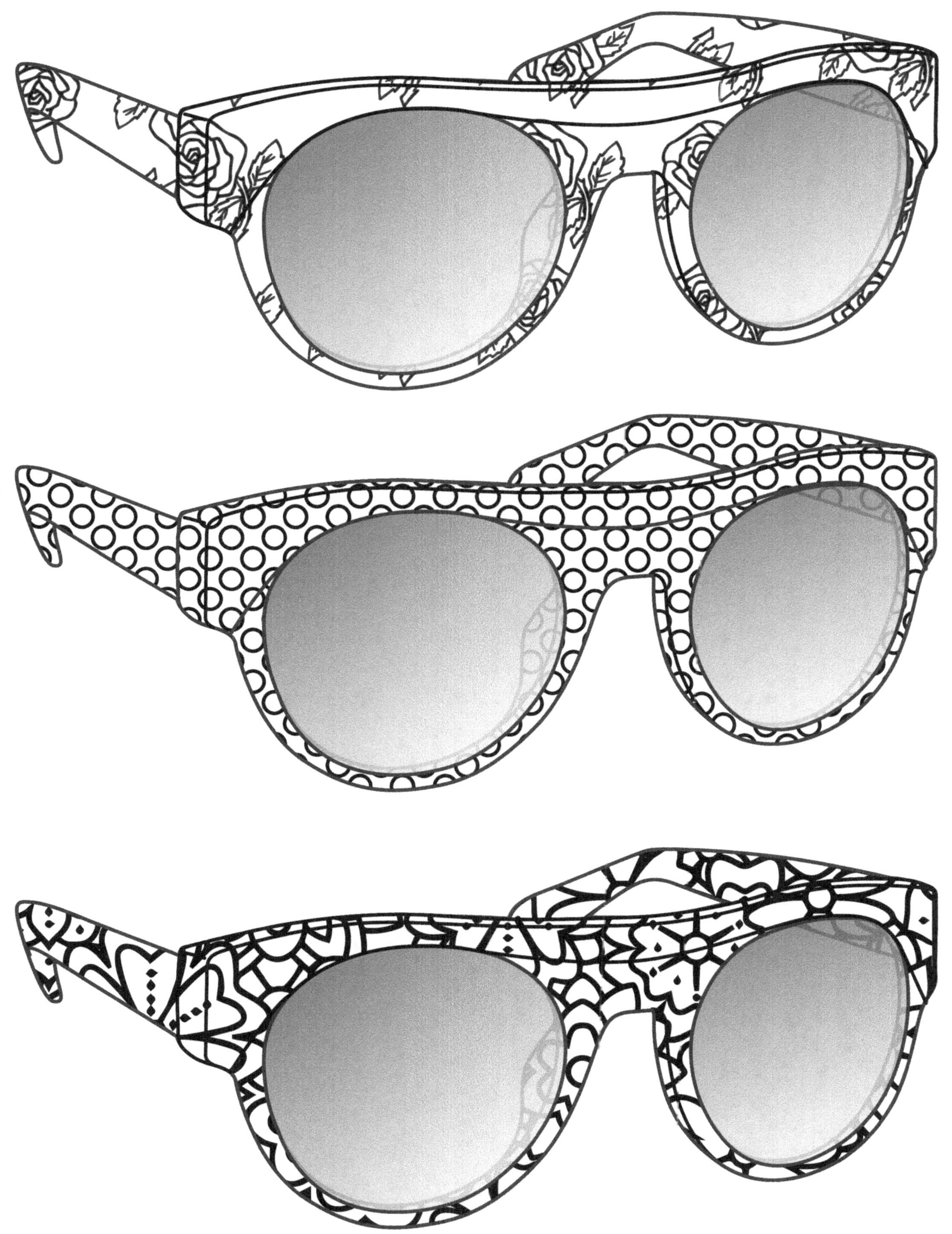

Decorate your own sunglasses!

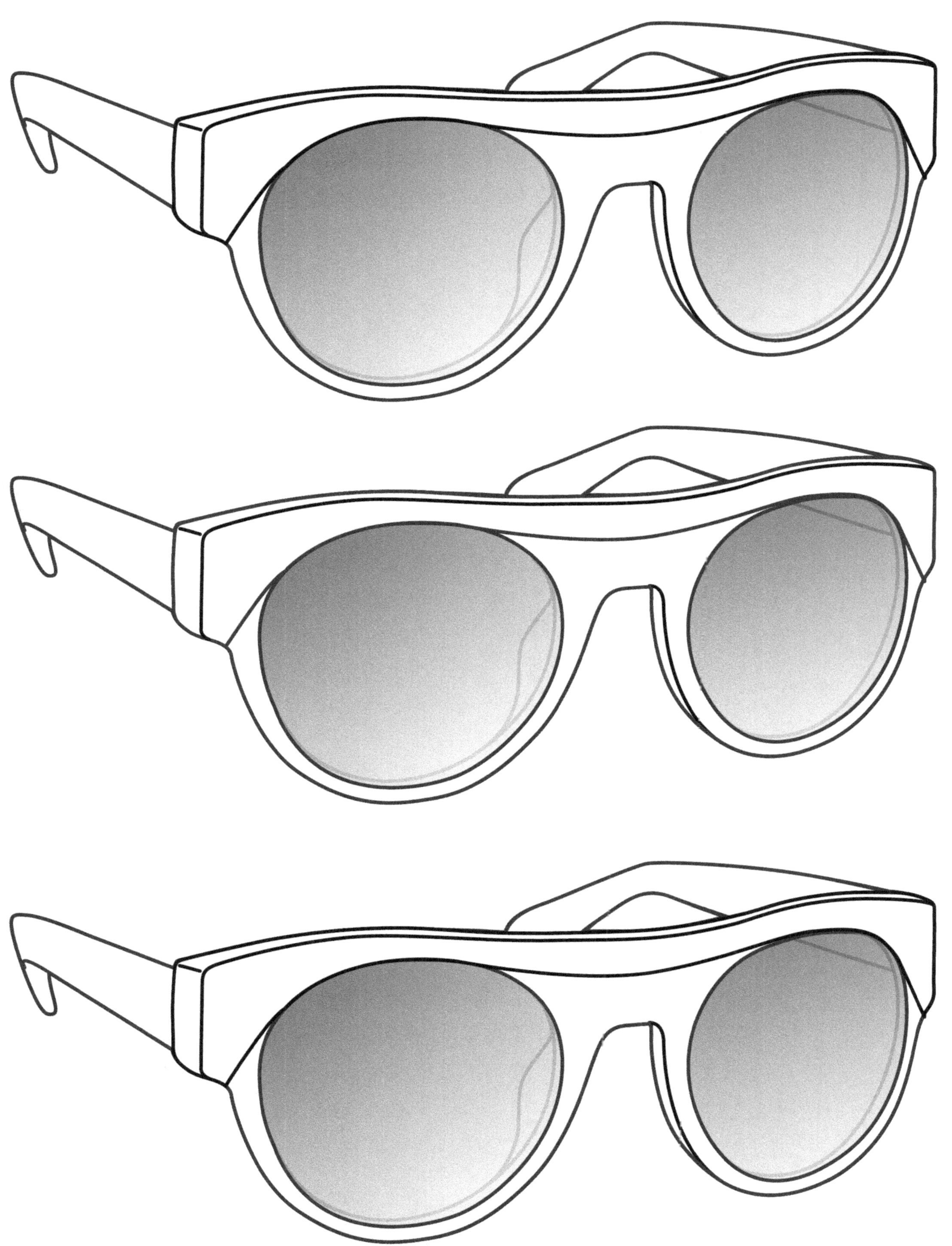

additional colorways
solid scrunchies
to match swimsuit

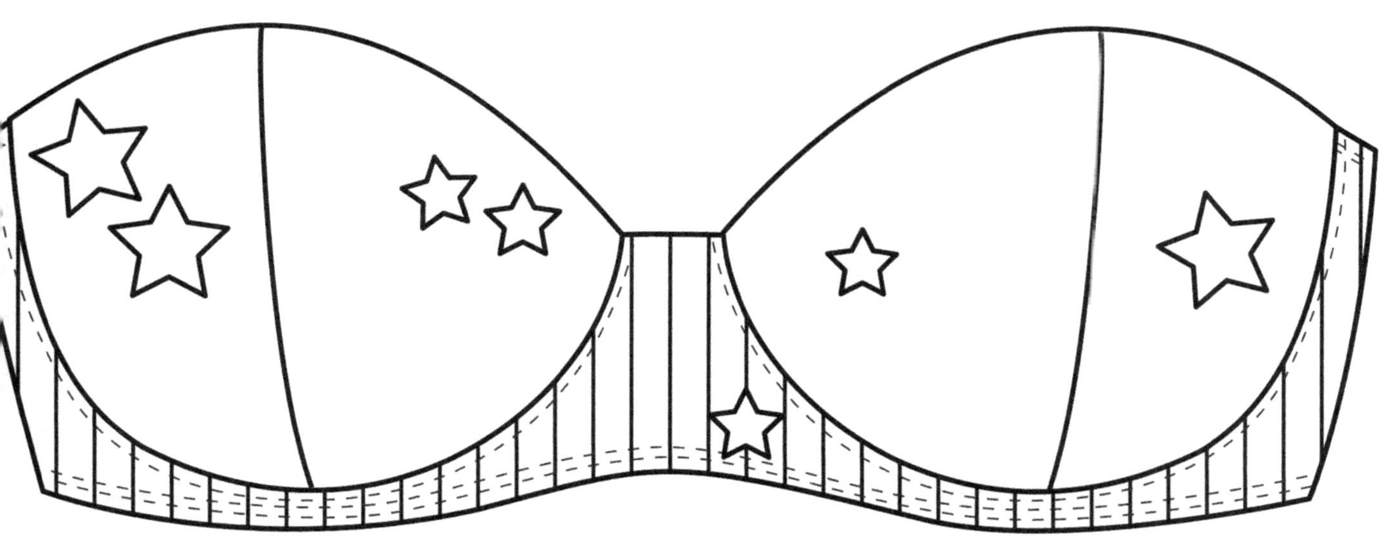

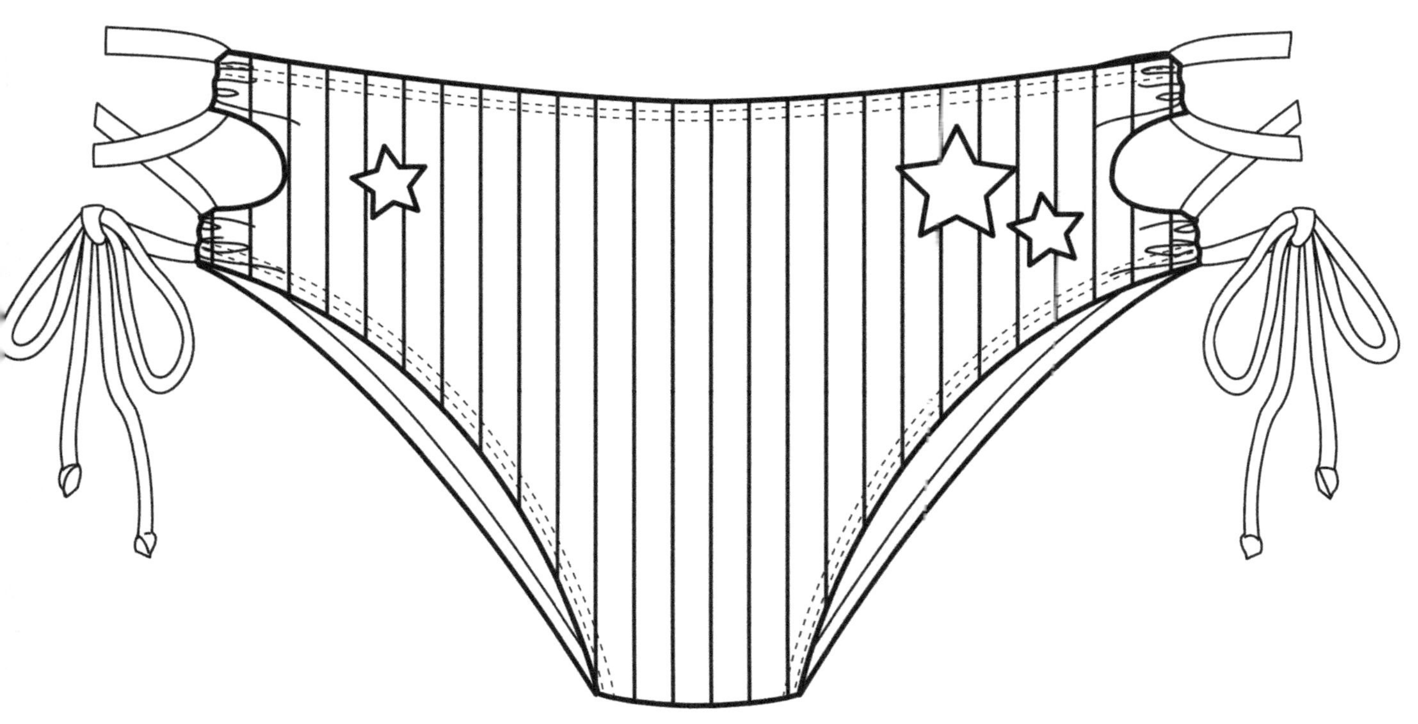

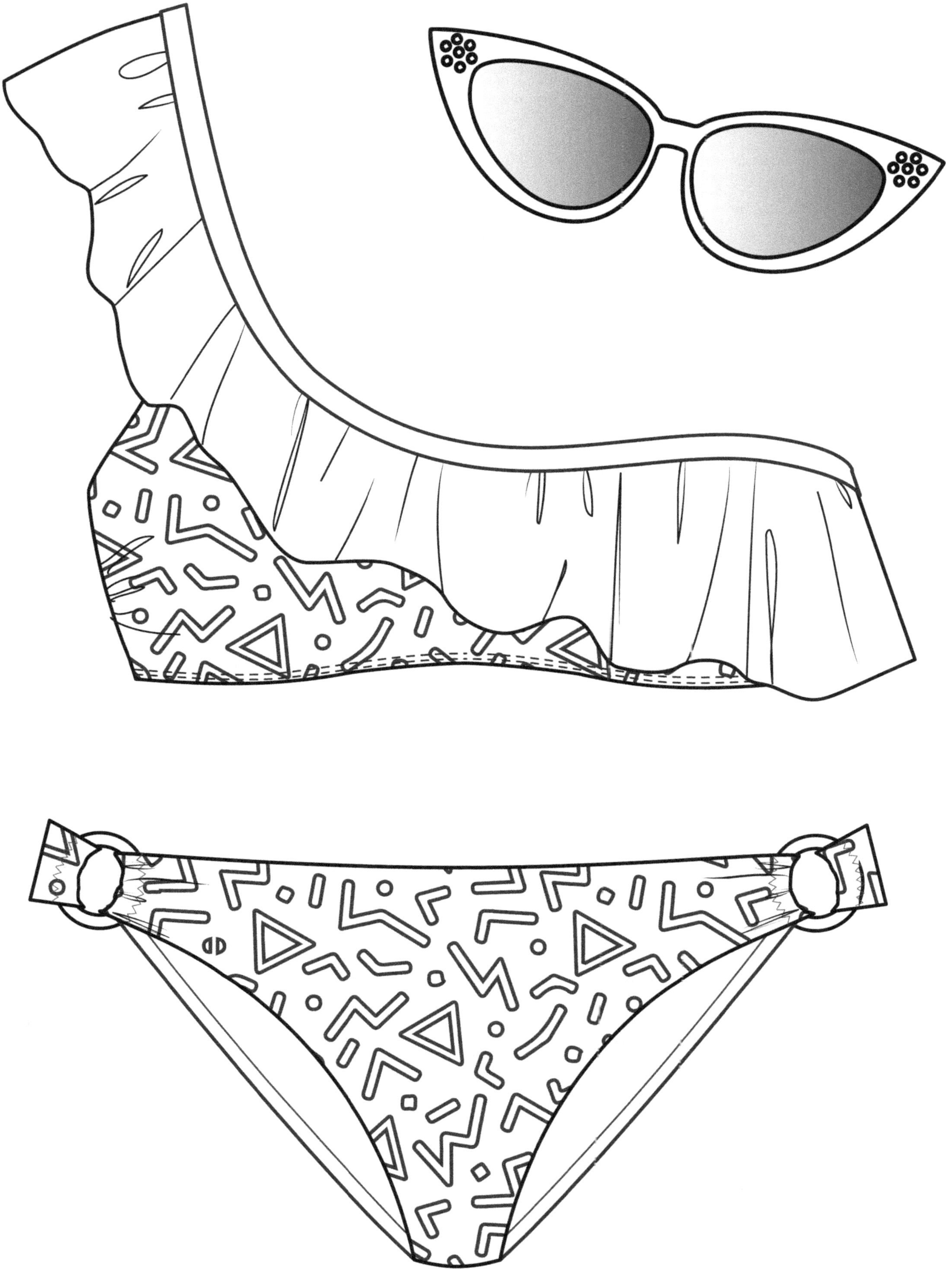

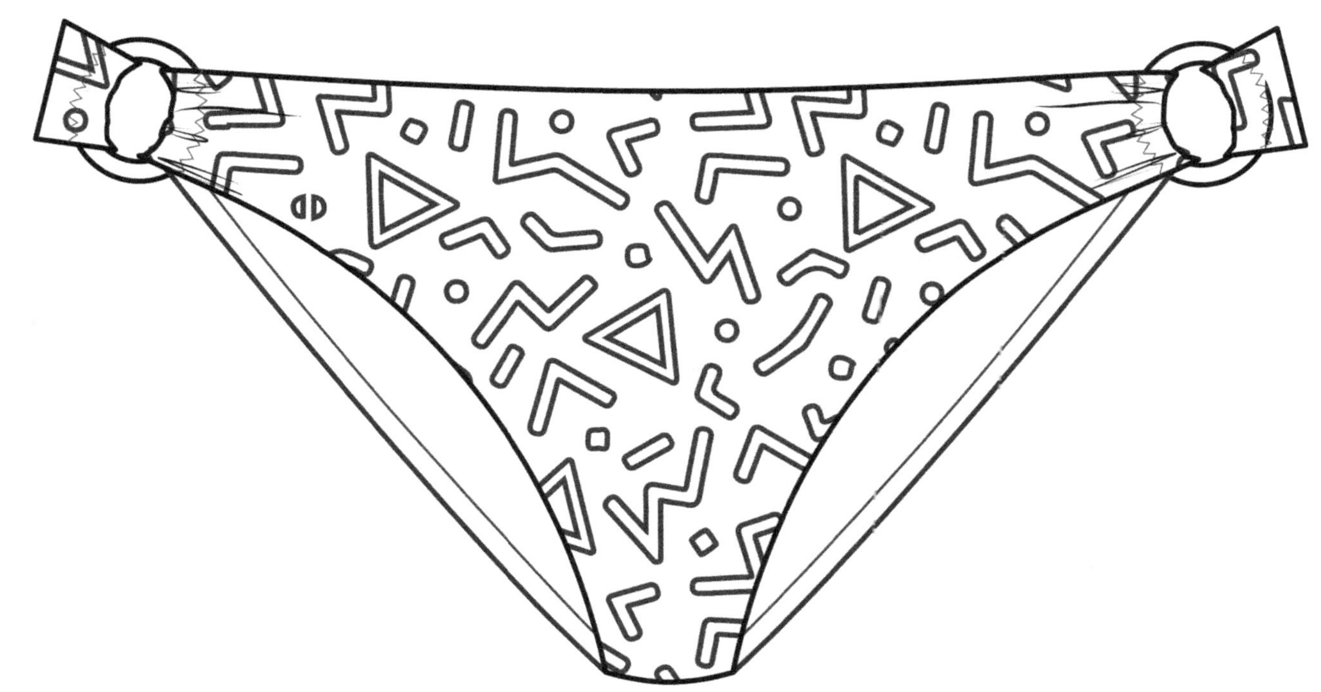

BEACH

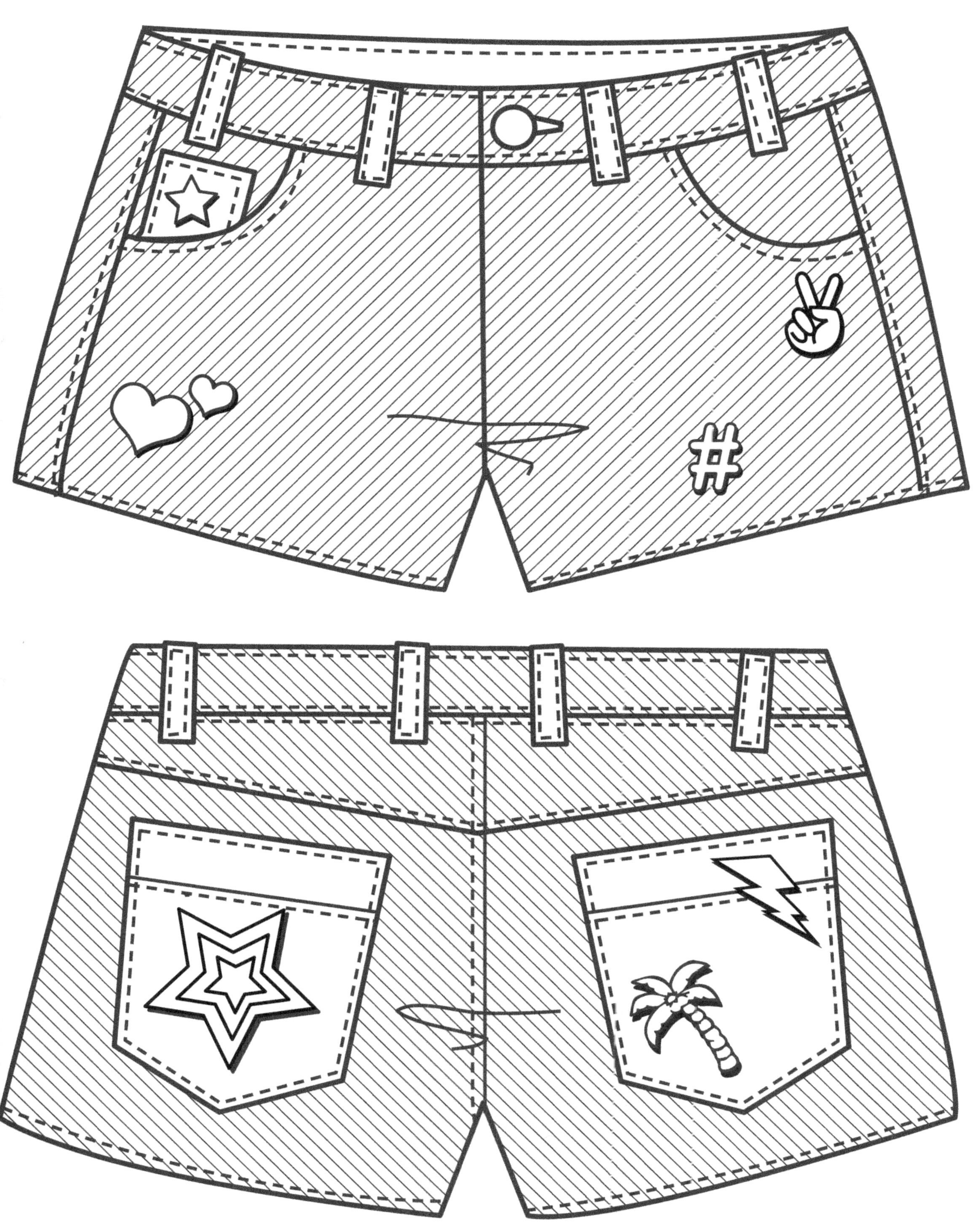

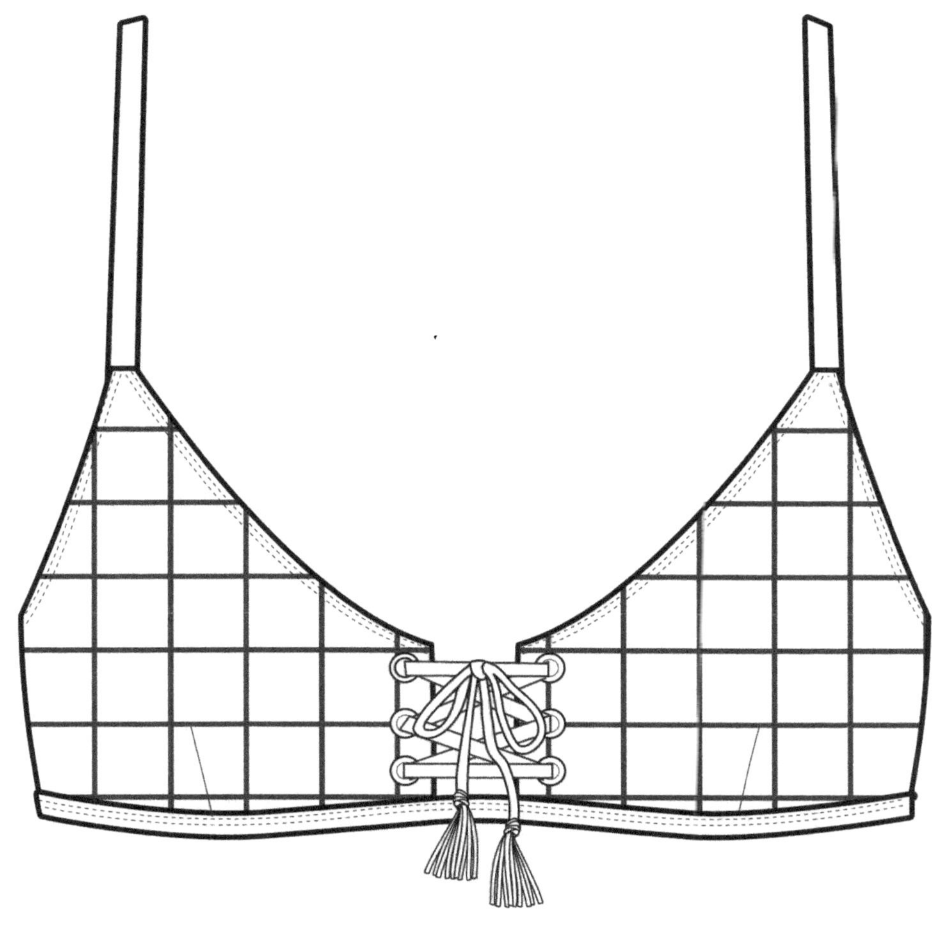

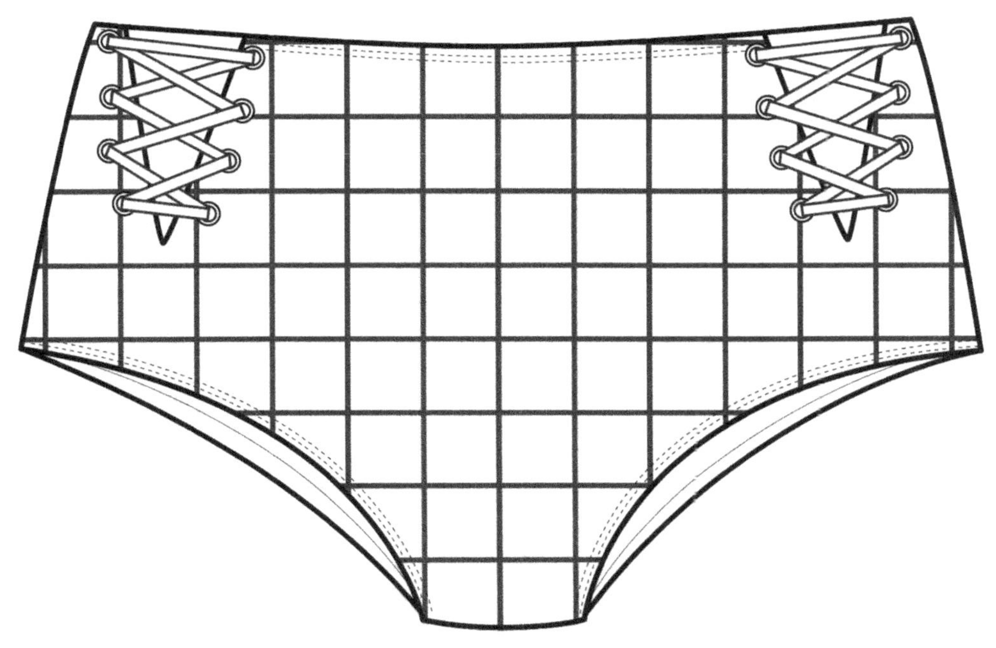

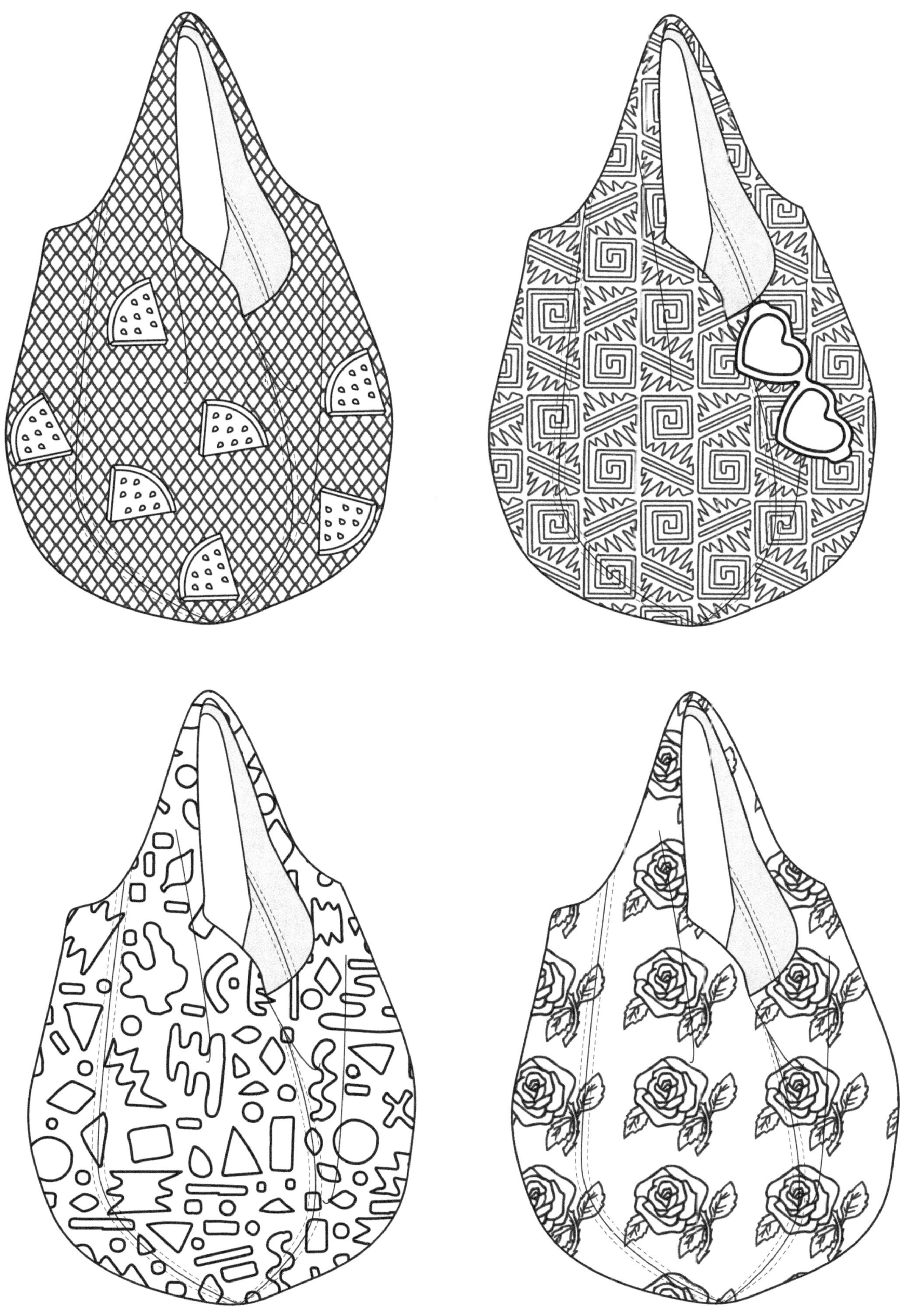

Design your own zip bags!

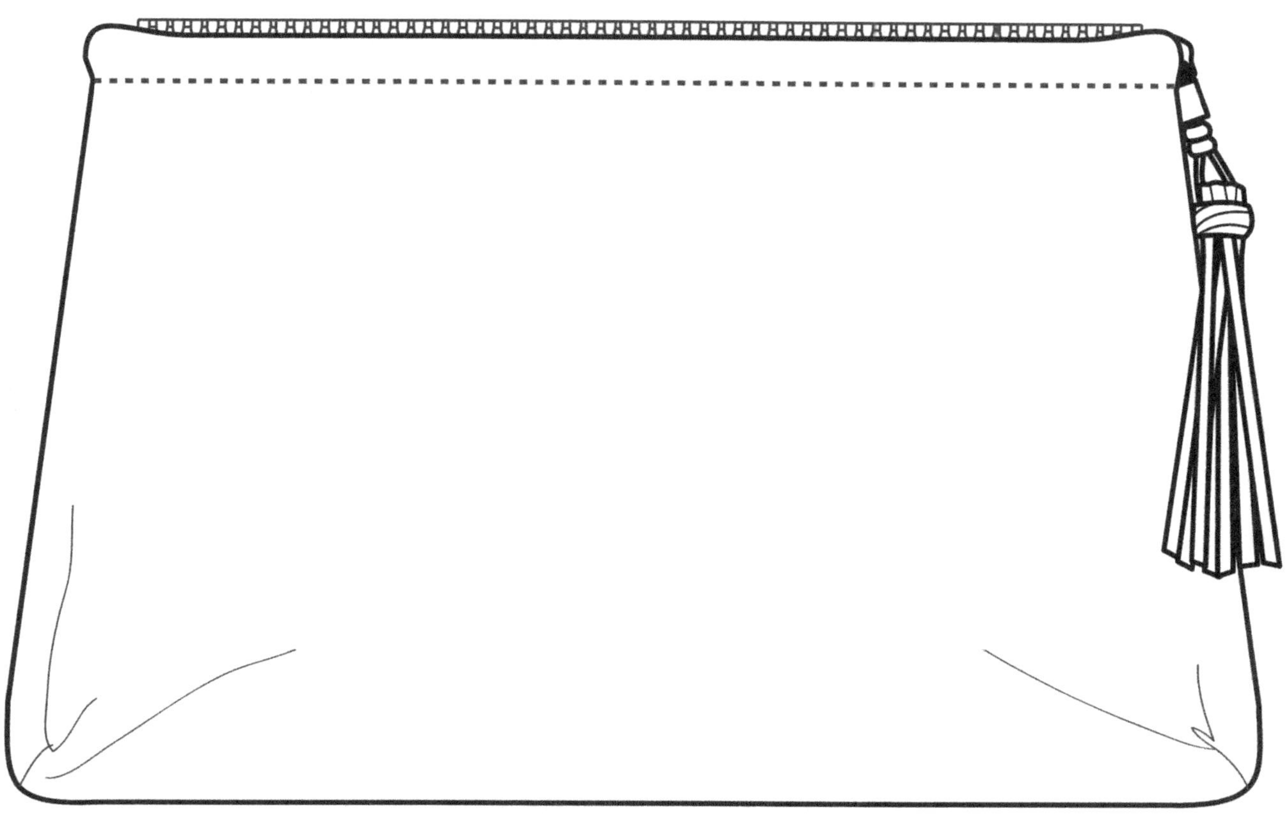

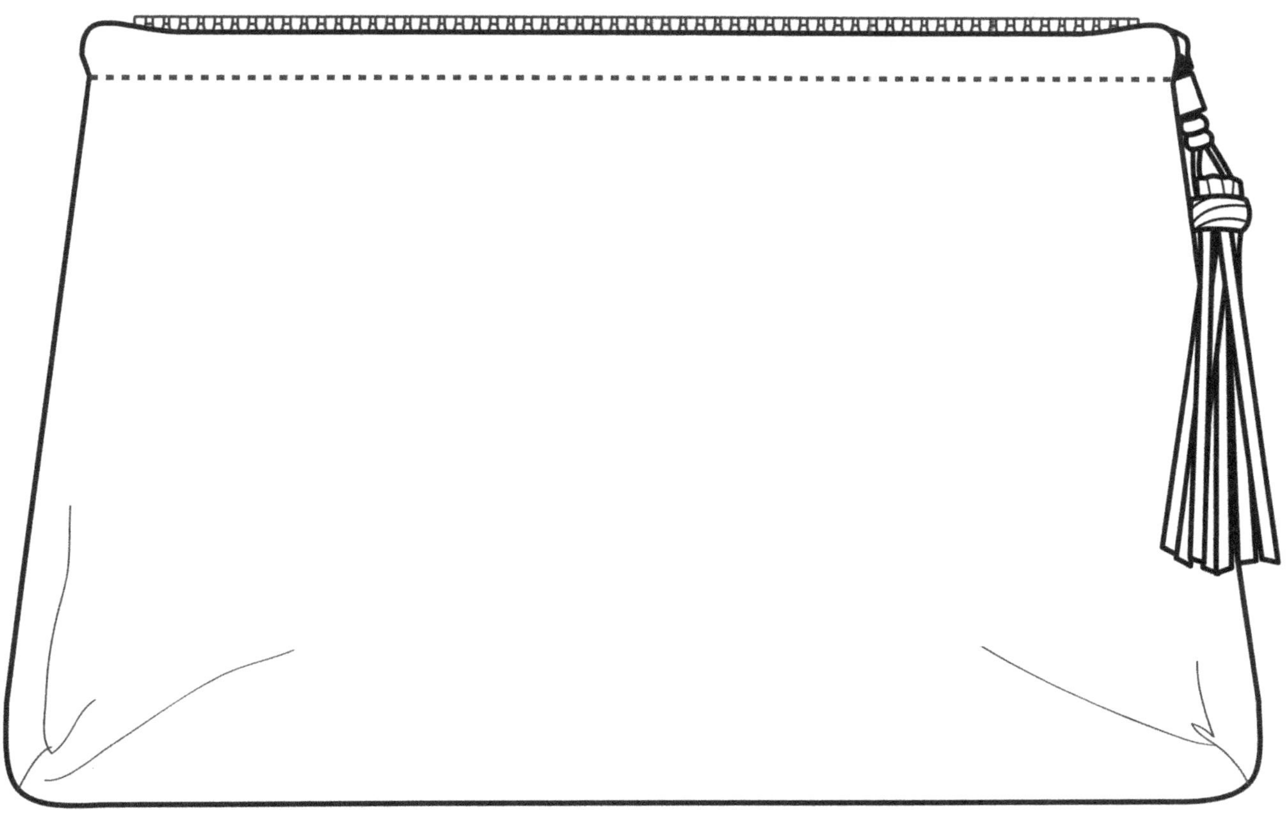

BEACH
VIBES

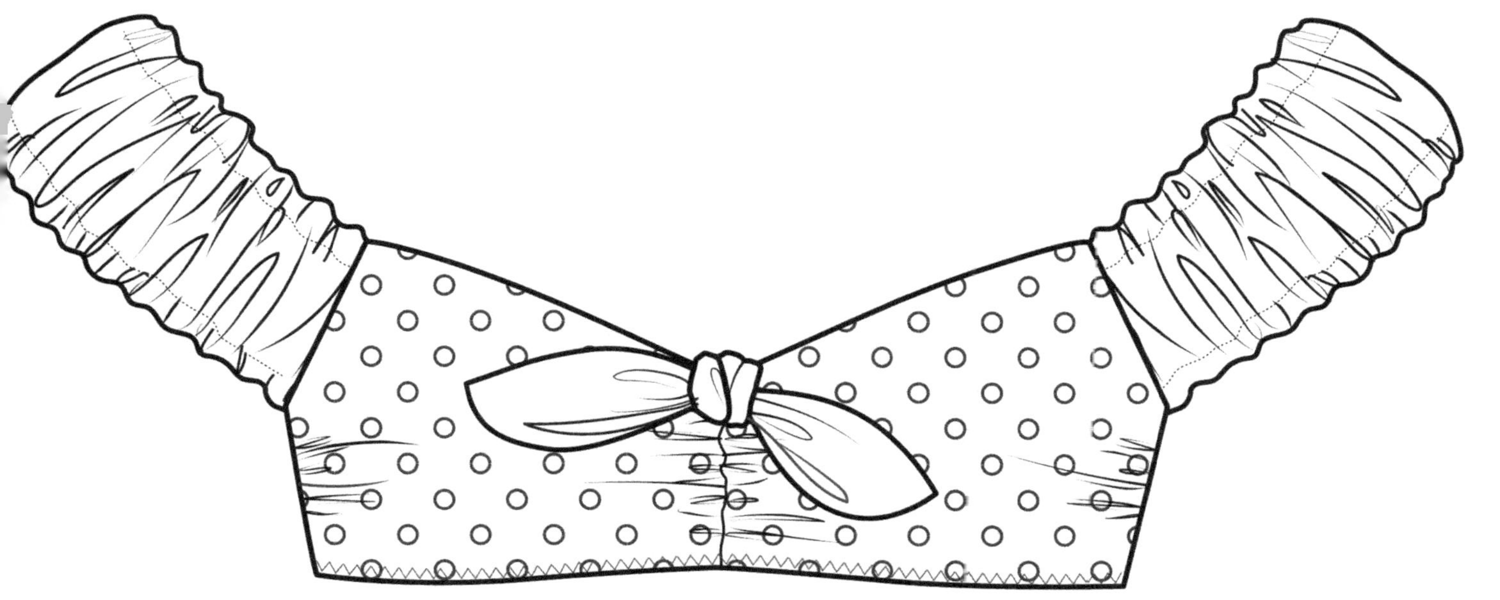
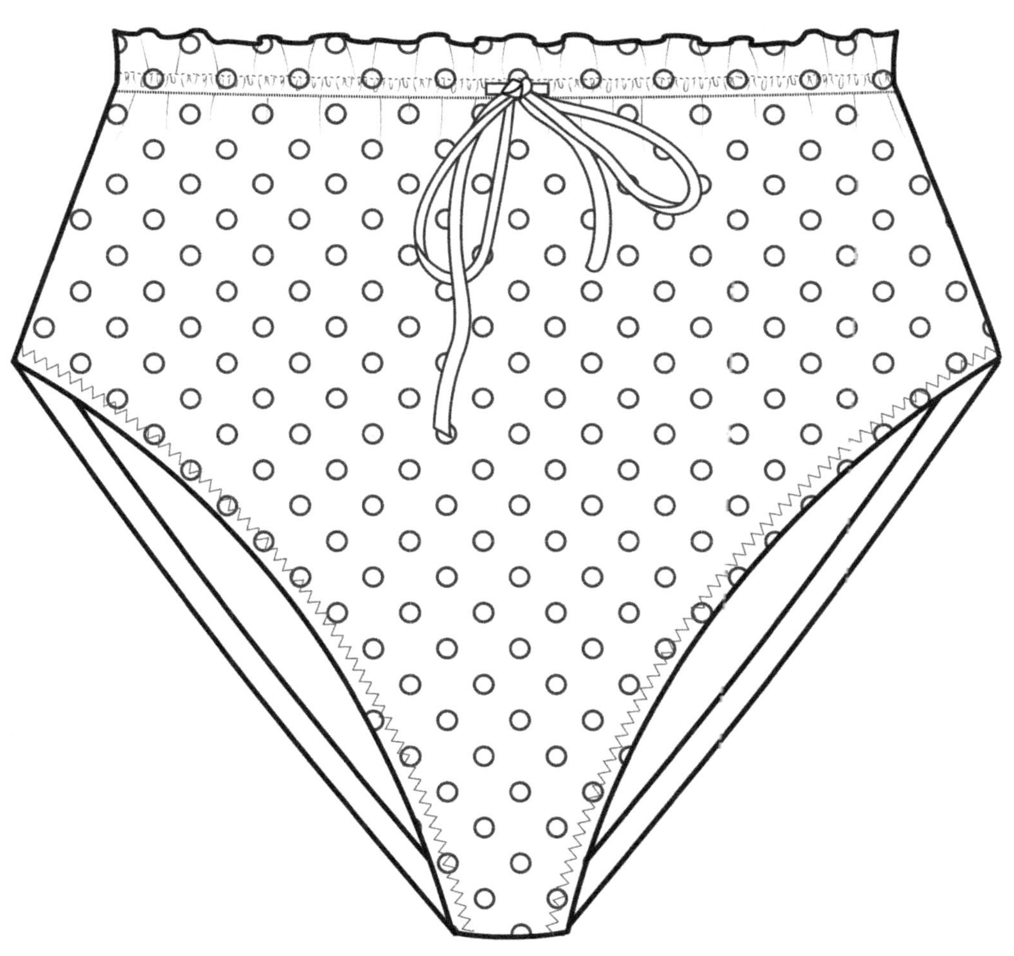

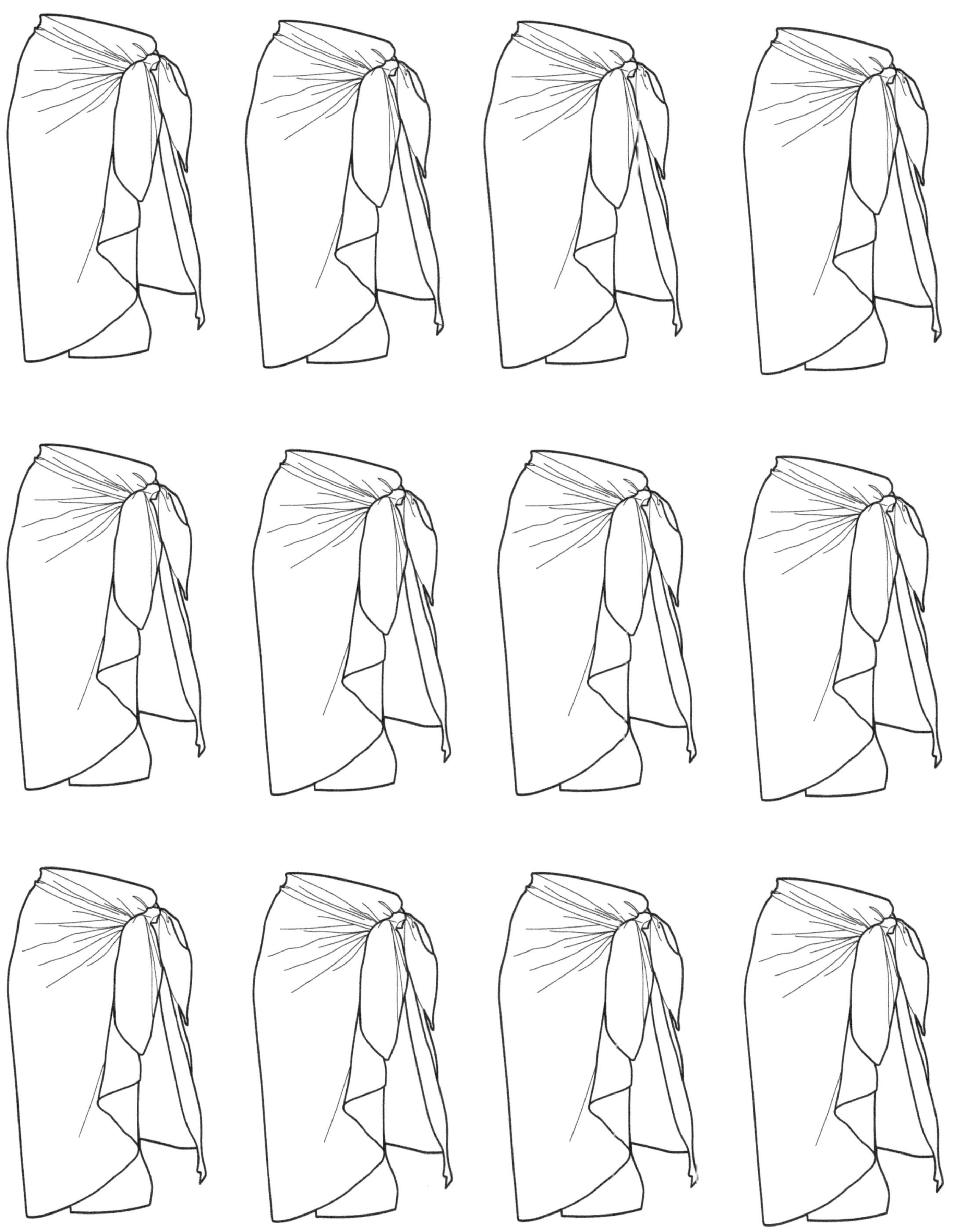

Design your own string bikinis!

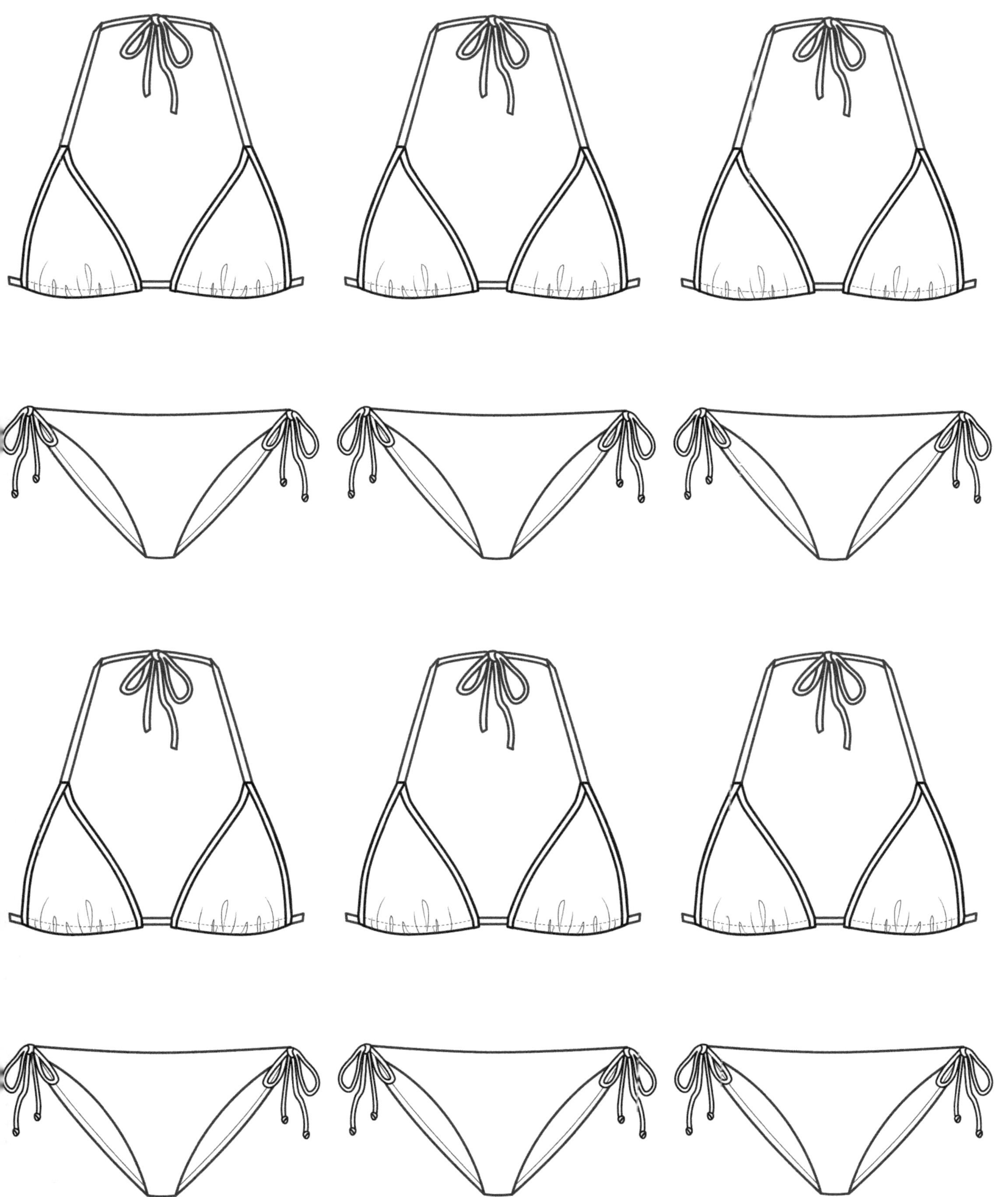